Miscellaneous Thoughts

Sandra Lugo

India | USA | UK

Presentation by *BookLeaf Publishing*

Web: www.bookleafpub.com

E-mail: info@bookleafpub.com

ISBN: 9789358313659

First edition 2023

To the friends in my day dreams - thank you for everything.

To my moral compass - thank you for believing in me.

PREFACE

I may be functional, but I'm not the most sane
person out there. My mind is usually clouded
with a fog of dread, uncertainty, and panic, even
in my happiest moments. There are many twists,
turns, and dead ends in my mind that are filled
with monsters and insane thoughts. It isn't
always pleasant walking through the labyrinth in
my head, so I usually keep my head in the
clouds.

Daydreaming can be such an amazing escape.
The beauty of fantasies sets my mind at ease, if
at least for a short while. Unfortunately,
intrusive thoughts make their way into my
daydreams about half the time. They add dark
turns, but at the very least, my dreams still end
in happiness or neutrality.

I love letting my daydreams unfold by
themselves. Though my demons can get the
better of me even in my dreams, I always feel at
ease knowing that even my insanity can't defeat
my longing for a happy (or at the very least,
neutral) life. Maybe, that will change in the
future. Maybe, it won't. Regardless, what

matters most to me right now is that despite the gloom and negativity everyone knows me for, my daydreams continue to be a happy place.

echoed silence

How I've been struggling
I can't put these thoughts behind me
I can't get the voices to stop
Make them stop

Their silence is loud
Their silence is deafening
Silence me now
Silence me forever

Mirrored in the reflection of your lively eyes
The ones I'll gladly die for
Overshadowed by the thoughts that won't leave
my head
The things the voices said

Gravity can't stop me
My mind drifts farther and farther each time
And I'm afraid it might be too late
Gather what is left of me
And drop it in the ocean
For no one to ever find again

It never got better
I never got better

If only you could hear
The deafening silence
So loud, the silence of the voices in my head
So loud, that the colors are gone
The last bit of joy left in this world
Is gone forever
And I can never get it back
The beautiful strokes of color
When I close my eyes
They're gone, and I will never see them again

I've fallen deep
While my mind leaves this world
Slowly
Maddening
Panicking

I can no longer sleep
I can no longer wake
I can't wait until the rest of me is gone

Sweet relief
Come to me
End this dream
Set me free

Dear Friend

Dear Friend,
Is it a fine day where you are?
Since you're always so far,
I can never think of things to say to you,
yet my mind explodes with thoughts going
through
waiting to be given to you,
but that is something I cannot do.
Every day,
I think of things to say,
but I can never speak.
The voice I need
doesn't exist,
so I am forever lost in a silent mist
with no way out.
electronic messages, a bond between us
particles and waves were all that it was
that thin bond that let me know you were still
there
with a fragile hope that you still care
yet I still hope for the impossible
while my thoughts are being interrupted like a
pebble
being thrown into a lake
as the water begins to shake

While the ripples slowly travel towards the edge
thoughts come and go
the late nights and the lack of sleep
it's all for something as I fall deep
into feelings that I can't keep.
I've gone completely blind
with the endless thoughts that race through my
mind.
What am I to do
if I ever see you again?
it can never be real
nothing I can ever feel
will ever be true,
and so I might never see you again.
What will happen one day?
Will we have nothing left to say?
Will our thin bond break?
nothing I can do
a hungry heart I cannot feed
a broken heart no longer beats
I can no longer carry on writing
as a dying soul can't keep on fighting,
and I pray that you will remember me
and never forget, as I won't forget you.

Sincerely,

Your Friend

to fall upon blind eyes

whenever time stands still
and everyone else won't care
you sit there wondering
why you're all alone
you sit there and think
of all the things you could have done differently
you sit there and wonder
what it is that you did so wrong
what it is they don't like
what it is that's wrong with you
knowing it's out of your control
knowing you can't fix it

I wonder if I'll ever meet anyone
who will make an attempt
someone who will listen
someone who will see me
and know that I'm not doing it on purpose
but everyone turns away
everyone walks away
and I'm left standing with a broken heart
a heart so alone and broken
a heart so empty
and no one will ever know
no one will ever listen

will anyone ever hear me
hear the deafening silence that pours from my
soul
the agonizing silence I've submitted to
that they've imposed on me
the burning quiet that comforts me
and puts me to sleep

I long for the day when nothing will matter
anymore
the day I can finally be at peace forever
to close my eyes, to finally rest
from the constant storm in my mind
the storm that won't let me surface
I long to sink to the very bottom
embracing the cold
embracing the darkness
and as the light would fade
so would my breath
and finally
I could be at peace with the silence
and it will be comforting
and I will be okay

Unreasonableness

I'm running as fast as I can
but I can't keep up
I'm running
I'm trying

It always seems to slip my grasp
missing by so little
I almost had it
but I always do
always
just barely
I'm trying

but can I make it?
Can I do it?
I reach out
as far as I can
as far as I can
is never far enough
I always fall short
just barely missing the mark
but I'm trying

I got out of bed
and that's as far as I got

I went to work
and that's as far as I'll ever get
I sit and write and mull over my life
and I'm trying
but is it enough?
I'm trying

I looked at the sky
and that's as far as I got
Intoxicated with the colors of the sunrise
it's a new day
and I'm still here
falling short
just missing the mark
and as I breathe in the morning,
I try for another 100 times
It never ends
but I'm trying

At the end of the rope,
who's there with me?
It's just me
That's what I get
for being the one that always misses the mark
the one that always falls short
I get left behind
and that's fine
I'm trying

I sit
I reflect
I sulk
I continue
one more failure
one more crash landing
one more wildfire
time and time again
one more wildfire
one more crash landing
one more failure
try, cry, sleep
and repeat
I'm still trying
it's useless
I'm still trying
regardless of outcome
I'm still trying
against all odds
but I'm trying

The Manic Lovers

The fascination you inspire in me
is almost terrifying
Everything about you is a marvel
and I am your humble worshiper
Loneliness is my religion
and you are my god
I can't save the world
so I'll gladly destroy it for you
My fellow demented
you and I
possess the insanity others can only dream of
You satiate my madness
and together, we can escape
and lose ourselves in each other's lunacy
in a delirious dream
What do you say?

silence speaks.

Silence speaks when words aren't enough for deaf ears that offer to listen. You give out a wordless speech. Your thoughts are a paintbrush to the canvas that is the world. Silence speaks when words aren't enough,

but right now, I don't have either.

Your Nothing

we sacrifice
what we don't have
give and take what we can get our hands on

your heart keeps beating
but your soul is dead
you replay memories
like a personal movie
to try to remember what you felt
back when
the shell you've become
slowly sinks to the bottom of another empty
bottle
and you begin to drown out
the entire world
as long as you get to see it
as the water fills your lungs
and you reach out
only to ignite
and burn into nothing
that the wind will blow away
what's around you is gone
and you're left in the dark
completely alone
you can't even move

and so you sit in silence
with no more memories to give
of the things you chose to disappear
of the relationships you dissolved
all alone in the nothingness
that is you

Empty World

a colorless page
suffocating smoke
the visions that I couldn't see
and the thoughts that yelled
louder than sirens

I can never return to the place where ghosts
mourn the living
as they remain living
oblivious to a world that will always be empty

when the streets quiet down
and the wind turns brisk
I see it
what haunts my days
the monster that hunts
for a soul as twisted
as macabre
as hypocritical
as mine

I don't move
because it looks into my eyes
blinding my reason
deafening my conscience

annihilating
the person I used to be

I can't go back to that place
it's long gone
it destroys what you hold dear
and it won't let go
ever again

Quiet Rooms

there is something about a quiet room
something that unsettles people
something that soothes me
away from noise
away from reason
away from the horrors of the world
when others fill you with light and sound
I embrace your silence
and your darkness
and your stillness
you bring me the clarity I need
for irrational decisions
and panic attacks
I love your isolation
I love your calm
I love your tempest
because only a quiet room
can truly understand

Calamity

Empty skies below
As I float away
Far away

Nothing in my grasp
I can't hold on
There's nothing in reach
Like sand slipping through my fingers
My dreams
They can't anchor me anymore
And I drift away

When did this
When did all of this
Slip from my grasp
My weakened hand
Can't hold on anymore
What cruelty
For life to take my love away

I sit among my tears and pens
And crumpled papers
And torn-up words
The failures of my past
The failures of my now

I can't believe it's come to this
A colorless life
And colorless sounds
And a blind soul

But no one cares
If it's not alive
No one cares
If it never lived
So dreams are mourned
In the silence of nothing
And people move on
But not me
For my heart is forever stuck
In the beautiful memories
Of my aspiration
Of my naivety
Of my dead and tired hope

I miss the days
I miss the nights
Of endless scribbling
Of endless doubt
Over every word
Every line
The days when I would write about nothing at
all
And the nights when I would write to the world
To the world that never saw

To the world that never heard
So empty
So silent
The letters I never sent
The letters you never read
The letters where I poured my heart out to you
The letters you never saw
The letters I never sent
So silent
So empty

A life plagued by "what if's"
What if
What if
A life plagued by something that doesn't exist
It turns into a world of madness
A world of nightmares
One where the corpses of my mangled dreams
Serve to flourish
To nurture
To encourage
A new line of dreams
And hopes
And "what if's"

And maybe this time
I won't be such a coward
Maybe I will
I never quite figured out

Just how it is that
I can keep such calamitous optimism
When I know I thrive in gloom
For that is all I am
Gloom
Uncertainty
And hopelessness

But I guess I'll never figure that out
And that's fine
I'll build it all up
From the dust and remains of the past
And when I'm finished
I'll burn it all down
With the flames of my passion
And end yet another "what if"
And then I'll start all over
And do it all again

Will this one be the one that makes it out?

Scream

I scream so loud
and I'm in so much pain
forever riddled with sadness and doubt
my mind will be
I feel I'm going insane
and I can't find the way back
to the calmer side of the storm
My heart is torn
between the desire to go on
and the incessant longing for sleep
sleep that will ease my mind
and momentarily free me from this insomnia
Oh, insomnia
How you make me question
my ability to find the willpower
that can save me
Every night, I mourn
the death of yet another piece of sanity
and hope
that could have kept me going
I'm so insane
and nobody knows
So insane
and desperate for someone to know

The Manic Lovers II

If I told you I'd never let go
would you stay?
My heart goes wild for you
and I'd do anything for you to stay
I'm not much
but I'm here to serve
and wait for you
like a stray cat
waiting to be pet
I don't quite have the words to describe it,
actually
but my love burns for you
like a wildfire
so out of control
and all for you
Anything and everything
for you

in the fallout

In the fallout
I see you
and you're beautiful
Like a lifesaver
you bring me up from the water
to breathe in some air
Like a monument
among the remnants of my shattered mind
I see you
and you are breathtaking
I reach out to you
and I hope you reach out to me
and never let go

the green room

24

The green walls of my room have seen so much.
They've watched the years go by and drag my
misery with them. It's a good thing walls can't
talk — the stories of my melancholy would
haunt anyone.

Ode to Insomnia

Insomnia
Oh, insomnia
Night after night, we meet
and we lay side by side
as you chase away my sleep
always keeping sight
of what goes on in my mind
You stick your hand into my thoughts
and create a tempest
thought after thought after thought
All night, when I lay to rest
you spin my thoughts
around and around and around
and it is beautiful
So wonderful
the sight of you
Every night
the only thing I can count on
You never leave me alone
You never cease
Night after night
you come, and you tease me
So lovely
to stir up ideas in my head
that never see the light of day

but you're there
always by my side
holding me in a tight embrace forever
and I love you

The voices laugh

So many voices
It's a little tough to know
what each of them want
but I can hear them
and I know what they want

I cry all night
I cry all day
and they laugh
They laugh at me
and humiliate me
and I sit there and take it
because I think I'm strong enough

They laugh at what I am
and what I was
and what I wanted to become
And they say things
mean things
things that make me cry all night
cry all day
My eyes are never cry
but I think I'm strong enough

Sometimes, I dream to escape

and I pretend to be happy
but they always make their way through
The voices
They turn my dreams into nightmares
and they torture me all day
and they torture me all night
and though my dreams prevail in the end
I'm still exhausted
and sad
and crying
every day, every night
and I wonder if I'm strong enough

Then the lovely sharp edges
they flirt with me
and they tell me I can be safe
so I pick one
and away we go
Replacing emotional turmoil
with painful bliss
So sharp and beautiful
but it fades so quickly
and I stare at the stains
in sadness and disappointment

And the voices laugh
and I cry
but maybe next time, I'll be strong enough

The Manic Lovers III

Take off the mask and face me
Look at who you truly are
in my expression
the one reflected in your eyes
Open your eyes and turn to me
I know you're scared
but I am so much crazier than you
and I can keep you safe
and I will love you forever
Please come with me
I won't ever let you go
If you just please take my hand
we can be crazy together
and love each other forever
The world will die around us
and it will be just us two
forever
What do you say?

cempasúchil

vibrant and alive
that's why you're a celebration of life
living in rich and bold colors
bouncing with life
and fragrance to calm the soul
you pull us in
to admire the sight of you
you bring us home
to where we belong
you are beauty
you are light
Aztec flower

the thought of you

the thought of you rings in my ears
your everything consumes me
I fall asleep to the thought of you
and when insomnia crawls into my bed
my head fills with the overwhelming desire
to say your name
to tell you what I feel
what I think
what to do
what am I to do
with the thought of you
endless thoughts that paralyze my will to get up
just so I can think of you
I fill my heart with your essence
as I reach out to you
never to be seen
or heard
or felt
I can only feel the fire inside me
that grows wild at the thought of you
and I beg for it to consume me
so I can burn for eternity
to the thought of you

Shawn Milke's voice

Lock my heart away
It's yours to keep
Your whispers overwhelm my incessant need for
love
Close my eyes
Your breath soothes my heart with every word
you speak
Come find me

Please return your gaze to me
For the minutes burn through me
It's so unbearable
So eternal

Meet my eyes
And I will take you to my dreams
Where our love blooms
Pretend that I'm normal

My heart is so heavy
My lungs are so heavy
I need you
Come to me
Please come to me

Put your hand in mine
Run away with me
And let my love paralyze you
Washing over you like a tempest at sea
Let my love disappear the world
Just you and me
Forever and ever
Let me love you infinitely
Like a dream
My dream
Never let go of me

Voice from the Soul

You
who I can only describe as art
You
the talent and charisma and humility

When the words you write
spill out to the world
the world listens
and it listens with joy
The words you write
and bring to life
with the enchantment of your melodies
they sneak across the air
and into our hearts
Like a breeze in the winter
to send chills down one's skin
So vivid, so alive
your words feel

Engraved into countless hearts
we sing the words
you bring to life
We breathe the music
that pours out from your soul
We live the dreams

you help us create
You are art

You see the world
and it sees you
Magnificent with skill
dressed in confidence
exuding warmth
The world is yours
and you deserve it

The fantasies your words create
live long and joyful
Even the hell in your works seems incredible
awe-inspiring
Breathe taking, you are
you and your works
from the pinnacle to the depths of insanity
you build worlds
and we live in them
and we prosper

The desire to envy you fades quickly
for it's difficult to hold resentment towards you
Though I would kill to stand on your pedestal,
I am fulfilled just looking at it
from afar,
enjoying the sight
of magnificence

and awe
and inspiration
And though sadness may poke at my back
when I think about it,
it is never enough
to dampen my admiration
even slightly

Your voice resonates loud and strong
and it takes hold of countless lives
Never letting go
for the words you spill echo throughout the
world
and we listen
We will always listen

I can only hope to have even a minute fraction
of what you give
so I can give it to you
in exchange for a brief second
of mutual appreciation and admiration
Just a second
just one
The curtains are always open for you
and the world
anxious to catch a glimpse
of your essence
You
who creates from the soul

who creates from passion
from the heart
from love
The skies are your canvas
and you fill them up
with paradises and infernos
And we watch
and we listen
to the voice calling out from your soul
We hear you